DISCOVERING TAROT with
Alan Dee Geddes

GLASS**SPIDER**PUBLISHING

Paperback ISBN: 978-1-957917-14-6
E-book ISBN: 978-1-957917-15-3

Library of Congress Control Number: 2022915811

Cover design by Judith S. Design & Creativity
www.judithsdesign.com
Published by Glass Spider Publishing
www.glassspiderpublishing.com

For Alasun, Zak, and Ricky

CONTENTS

INTRODUCTION

I have always been fascinated with sleight of hand magic. As a teenager during the late seventies, I would often visit The Fun Shop, a magic and novelty store in Ogden, Utah. It was there that I also discovered my first Tarot deck, an early version of the Waite-Smith deck. The magician on the box, and the four aces with hand illustrations similar to those found in conjuring textbooks, had me sold immediately!

I would often dabble with Tarot, but it was not until 1996 that I chose Wicca as my spiritual path. One of the teachings of Wicca is to acquire a magickal tool. That was the inspiration I needed. I've been reading Tarot cards professionally ever since.

The contents of this book is based upon a series of revised lecture notes from Tarot classes I have taught throughout Utah for over twenty years. I've also included new chapters and sections on the associations of Tarot as applied to other modalities.

Thank you for your interest in my work!

Sincerely,
Alan Dee Geddes

CHAPTER 1
The Fool's Journey Meditation

The twenty-two cards of the Major Arcana have special meaning. When read in order, a mystical journey unfolds.

We begin the first phase of our journey as **The Fool**, a disembodied spirit who is dead and yet unborn.

As we incarnate into the material plane, we become **The Magician**, furnished with the elements of earth, air, fire, and water. These are energies we manipulate and are a part of.

In **The High Priestess**, Virgin Daughter of the moon, we represent the hidden connection between spirit and material. We are the eternal feminine.

As **The Empress**, we become Earth Mother, fertility of all life. Through us, we represent the passive, the nurturer, and the subconscious.

As **The Emperor**, we become Earth Father, seed of all life. Through us, we represent the aggressive, the protector, and the conscious.

In **The Hierophant**, or High Priest, we embody the external form of religion and tradition. We are the eternal masculine.

Among **The Lovers**, we find connection between subconscious and consciousness. Choice, attraction, love, and healing are among the aspects of this archetype.

As we advance to **The Chariot**, having attained direction, we are able to steer readily through this plane. We have reached an outer triumph.

In the second phase of our journey, we incorporate **Strength** to provide balance between spiritual and carnal nature, creating harmony amid opposing forces.

Focusing on spiritual nature, we become **The Hermit**. The internal light we encounter is that of self-awareness, as symbolized by a glowing lantern.

Wheel of Fortune represents the game of life. Applying the law of attraction, we have the ability to create good luck by positive action, or bad luck by negative action.

In **Justice**, we contemplate the scales of balance. Delving deeper, we become truly aware of our actions and what effect they encompass in the future.

The Hanged Man represents our willingness to make a sacrifice for greater spiritual understanding. As we bear the symbolic cross of salvation, we discover new paths for healing our soul.

Having had spiritual awakening, we are now ready to let go and allow **Death** to transform us, abolishing negative energy, and opening up channels for positive energy.

In **Temperance**, we have encountered our guardian angel, who teaches us the secret of transforming spirit from the subconscious into the activity of consciousness.

On the third and final phase of our journey, we arrive at **The Devil**, ever reminding us of negative energy. We all have free will to change.

Through **The Tower**, we find a powerful equalizing force, destroying all unbalanced energy. This is a radical change that brings enlightenment.

A new truth shall unveil itself in silence as **The Star**. It is through meditation that we find insight, inspiration, and hope.

We now have a deeper ability to connect with Goddess energy and all of Her aspects as reflected by **The Moon**.

Likewise, we have a deeper ability to connect with God energy and all of His aspects as illuminated by **The Sun**.

Judgment is the reawakening of nature under influence of spirit—the mystery of birth, death, and rebirth. Through our effort and suffering, we have uncovered the secrets of life.

And finally, we arrive at **The World**, which brings us back to spirit. We have attained our gift of cosmic consciousness as we dance the dance of life in the center of the universe.

CHAPTER 2
The Celtic Cross Spread

The history of the Celtic Cross Spread suggests it originated in Europe. It is believed to be a modification of earlier spreads which were laid out in the form of a cross.

Probably the first published reference to this spread was in 1910 in the book *The Pictorial Key to the Tarot* by Arthur Edward Waite, where he called the spread "an ancient Celtic method of divination."

Waite makes reference to the Celtic Cross Spread and describes it as a short process that has been used privately for many years past in England, Scotland, and Ireland. Waite also states that, to his knowledge, this spread has not been published in any other form before, and certainly not in connection with Tarot cards.

We know that members of the Hermetic Order of the Golden Dawn, of which Waite was a member, used this spread. The Golden Dawn was a magickal occult order based in Great Britain that was active during the late nineteenth century and the early part of the twentieth century.

As you study this spread, published in many sources, you will discover that there are many variations. Positions, as well as definitions, will differ from author to author—however, the basic structure remains the same.

Through my years of reading Tarot cards, I too have modified the positions and definitions of the Celtic Cross Spread.

My Interpretation

Begin by having the cards shuffled. As the querent is shuffling, ask them to take a couple of deep breaths to focus and center, and to think of a question, or suggest they clear their mind for a general reading.

The shuffling method I use is called the Mud Pie or Wash, which means spreading the cards face down on the table to mix. This is an excellent way of putting energy into the cards. While the querent is shuffling, if one or two cards fly out of the deck or turn face up, I always keep them because they make excellent clarifier cards.

After reassembling the cards, have the querent cut the deck with their left hand and complete the cut. (The left hand is closest to the heart!) This brings the significator card to the top and the shadow card to the bottom of the deck.

The significator card represents the querent. Finding it by shuffling the deck is my preferred method. It acts as a gauge on how accurate the reading will be. You may also have the querent select their own. Court cards are traditionally used in this process.

Next, verify the orientation of the deck (which end is up) if you read cards in reverse. I'll have more on reversed cards later on in this chapter.

Note: As you deal the cards, turn each one face up as you would turn the page of a book—in other words, side by side. If you turn them end over end, you'll be reversing their position. A lot of books on Tarot that I've read over the years don't cover this important detail. Keep this in mind to ensure you know which end is officially up!

*For placement of cards, see the illustration at the end of this chapter.

Significator Card

Deal the significator card face up on the table and share its meanings with the querent. Afterward, deal the following twelve cards to form the spread.

CARD ONE: Present Situation

This card represents the situation the querent is currently in. It reflects the atmosphere in which they're living and working. Place this card on top of the already dealt and tabled face-up significator card, about halfway to the lower right.

CARD TWO: Influencing Factors

This card represents the influencing factors of the situation at hand. It is read at the top right so that reversed meanings can be applied. Place it across card one, top end to the right.

CARD THREE: Hopes

This card represents the hopes of the client; their ultimate goal or destiny. If this card is negative, it could represent an acknowledgment of a situation that can be changed for the better. Place it above the cross.

CARD FOUR: Recent Past

This card represents energies that are just passing and still being incorporated into the querent's present situation. Lessons still being learned. Tempering future strength. Place it to the right of the cross.

CARD FIVE: Distant Past

This card represents situations that existed in the past that have been incorporated by the querent into the present. Future actions based on past experiences. A foundation of strength. Place it below the cross.

CARD SIX: Future Influences

This card represents energies that will be approaching in the near future. It represents the atmosphere in which future events will be influenced. Incorporating new energy. Place it to the left of the cross.

CARD SEVEN: Fears

This card represents fear of change and the unknown. An acknowledgment. If this card is positive, it could mean that the querent feels unworthy or has low self-esteem. Place it to the lower-right side of the completed seven-card cross.

CARD EIGHT: Environmental Factors

This card represents day-to-day living. Aspects the querent feels comfortable sharing with the outside world. Keeping up appearances. Fitting in. Thinking with the head. Sun energy. Place it above card seven.

CARD NINE: Inner Emotions

This card represents the querent's inner emotions and secret desires that are mostly kept private from the outside world. Gut feelings. The real person inside. Thinking with the heart. Moon energy. Place it above card eight.

CARD TEN: Possible Final Outcome

This card represents a combination of both positive and negative energies of the spread to form a possible final outcome. Place it above card nine to complete the staff.

CARD ELEVEN: Clarifier Card

This card is positioned on top of the deck after ten cards have been dealt. It represents aspects that can provide clarification. An embellishment to the structure. Place it to the left of card three.

CARD TWELVE: Shadow Card

This card is the one on the bottom of the deck. It describes the hidden dimensions of the subconscious that underpin the situation. Place it to the left of card five.

Timespans

The "V" formation of cards five, four, and six focuses on timespans.

Position 5 represents the distant past, which can represent a timespan of a year or more. It indicates a foundation of strength.

Position 4 represents the recent past, which can represent a timespan of three to six months. It indicates energies we are still incorporating into our life.

Position 6 represents the future influences that can represent a timespan of three to six months. It indicates energies to acknowledge and take advantage of.

Hopes and Fears

When I initially made a concentrated effort to study Tarot in 1996, the book *A Complete Guide to the Tarot* by Eden Gray (1970) was one of my first, and it remains one of my favorites. In Gray's version of the Celtic Cross Spread, the positions of hopes and fears are separated. Most published versions have the hopes and fears positions combined. I prefer the separation of the two, as previously explained in my interpretation of the spread.

Thoughts on reversed cards

I have read many books on Tarot through the years and have found that a lot of authors tend to apply mostly negative definitions to cards that show up in reverse. I believe many cards have a positive meaning in reverse.

There are also those who only read cards right side up because they feel there's enough positive/negative information in the deck, so reverse meanings aren't necessary.

I read cards in reverse, but I believe the upright meaning is the predominant one. When in reverse, I apply additional layers of interpretation. The artwork of the cards in reverse can also add additional information.

It's a personal choice. There is no right or wrong way to read the cards, provided there is consistency in your approach.

The Bigger Picture
I always look at the overall spread to discover additional important information. For example...

Ratio of Suits
Many Wands can represent a focus on physical energy and action. Many cups can represent a focus on feelings and emotions. Many Pentacles can represent a focus on financial, material, and practical concerns. Many Swords can represent a focus on thought processes and intellect. An approximately equal number of suits in the spread can represent the querent living a balanced life.

Missing Suits
If there's an absence of a particular suit in the spread, it can represent energy that doesn't need to be addressed since it's already being incorporated by the querent. Missing suits can also represent an energy to be acknowledged if the cards suggest that message.

Major Arcana Cards
A high ratio of Major Arcana cards in the spread can indicate many issues going on in the querent's life, resulting in a lack of focus. Fewer Major

Arcana cards can represent more focus, which makes the path easier for the querent to follow.

As part of the reading, I will always see how many of the Major Arcana cards show up, and in no particular order, I blend their meanings to tell a story about the spread. It's a great technique to summarize the message of the cards.

Reversed Cards
A high ratio of reversed cards can represent an acknowledgment, a blockage, or a dissipation of energy. Keep in mind that reversed cards can also have positive meanings, as mentioned earlier.

Right Side up Cards
A high ratio of right side up cards can suggest channels opening up, giving the querent a green light to move forward.

Other Observations
Lay out the cards so that both you and the querent can view the spread right side up.

Lay Position Three at the top and deal clockwise, as opposed to dealing counterclockwise.

Read the cards in the following order: significator; positions one and two; positions five, four, and six; positions three and seven; positions eight, nine, and ten; and last but not least, positions eleven and twelve.

In total, this is a thirteen-card spread. (I like the number thirteen!)

I always suggest that the querent take a picture of the spread with their smartphone so they can refer to it later, perhaps over a cup of coffee.

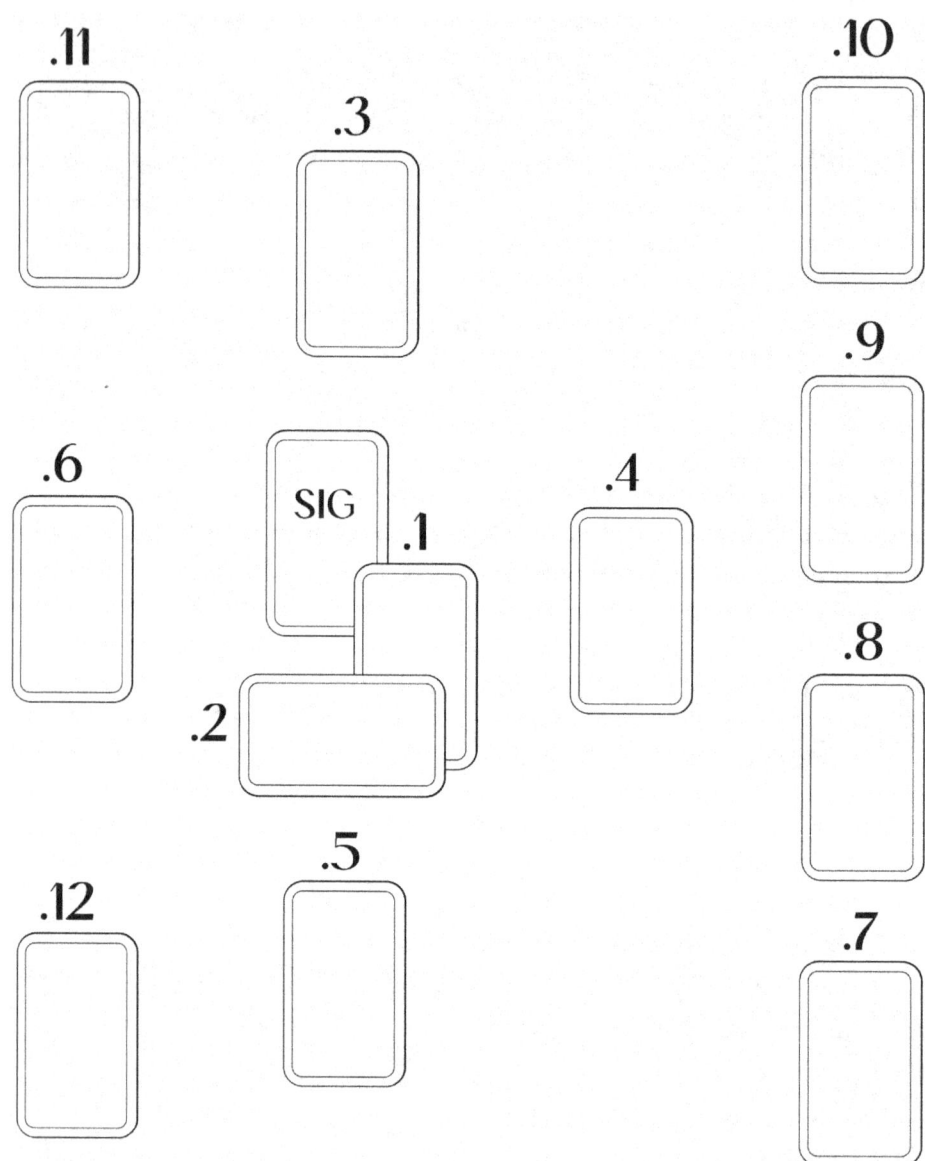

CHAPTER 3
Vision Spreads

Vision Spreads is a concept I came up with after studying vision boards. A vision board is a tool used to help clarify, concentrate, and maintain focus on a specific life goal. It can be any sort of board on which you display images that represent whatever you want to be, do, or have in your life.

In my Vision Spread, I apply the qualities of a vision board to my interpretation of the Celtic Cross Spread.

You can incorporate all seventy-eight cards in the deck, however I suggest it be comprised of seven Major Arcana cards. Aim for a balance between the Major and Minor Arcana.

The number seven represents contemplation, spirituality, and mastery.

This is a thirteen-card spread.

The number thirteen also has special meaning because the thirteenth card of the Major Arcana is Death, which represents change and transformation.

You will find my Vision Spread and interpretation at the end of this chapter.

Thirteen Vision Qualities

1- Health

2- Happiness

3- Wellness

4- Comfort

5- Peace

6- Security

7- Family

8- Relationships

9- Success

10- Financial Freedom

11- Wealth

12- Luxury

13- Vacations

Procedure

To begin, spread out all the cards of your favorite Tarot deck on the table. It's a good idea to put them in numerical order for easier reference. Next, go through each position and pick a card that represents your intent, and build the spread. Reverse cards may also be used. Keep in mind the thirteen vision qualities.

Significator Card

This card represents your ultimate self. Pick one that illuminates that aspect. It could be a Major Arcana card, or you could select a court card, which is often used to represent the qualities of the querent. Of course, any of the Minor Arcana cards can be used.

CARD ONE: Present Situation

This card represents the positive energy you're connected with and want to develop further. Place this card on top of the already dealt and tabled face-up significator card about halfway to the lower right.

CARD TWO: Influencing Factor

This card represents the crosscurrents in your life and positive influencing factors that keep you interested in the path you're on. Place it across card one, top end to the right.

CARD THREE: Hopes

This card represents your ultimate goal or destiny. What do you daydream about? Place it above the cross.

CARD FOUR: Recent Past

This card represents energies that are just passing and still being incorporated into your life, and important positive decisions you've made. Place it to the right of the cross.

CARD FIVE: Distant Past

This card represents past events that have been transformed into positive energy. Future actions based on past experiences. Place it below the cross.

CARD SIX: Future Influences

This card represents the positive energy you want to incorporate into your immediate future. Projects to start in readiness for future goals. Place it to the left of the cross.

CARD SEVEN: Fears

This card represents acknowledgments. Fear of change and the unknown. Discovering your deficiencies and determining the best way to address them. Place it on the lower right side of the completed seven-card cross.

CARD EIGHT: Environmental Factors

This card represents how you want to present yourself to other people. Your best outward appearance. Radiating positive energy in your own unique way. Place it above card seven.

CARD NINE: Inner Emotions

This card represents the reflection of your inner emotions and secret desires. Energies that resonate in your heart. Inspiration and creativity. Your authentic self. Place it above card eight.

CARD TEN: Possible Final Outcome

This card represents a combination of all the cards in the spread to achieve your ultimate goal—the end result of connecting with what you love, and taking action to make your dreams come true. Place it above card nine complete the staff.

CARD ELEVEN: Clarifier Card

This card is the one on top of the deck after ten cards have been dealt. It represents a positive overview of the spread, which can complement its meaning as a whole. It is an embellishment to the structure. Place it to the left of card three.

CARD TWELVE: Shadow Card

This card is the one on the bottom of the deck. It represents the positive energy that is part of your subconscious—something to discover and acknowledge. Place it to the left of card five.

In Conclusion

When you're finished, take a picture of this spread with your smartphone for ongoing inspiration. Another good idea is to place it upon a decorated altar. This concept can be applied to your favorite Tarot spread. Selected Tarot cards may also be incorporated onto a vision board.

My Vision Spread and Interpretation

Significator Card: The Magician
This is an obvious choice for me since I am a magician in the conjuring arts as well as a magician in the spiritual sense.

CARD ONE: Present Situation = Temperance
This is the card, Pamela Colman Smith's artwork, that I have on the cover of my *Book of Shadows*. I believe it was Archangel Michael that inspired me to quit drinking alcohol. This is the same card that shows up in my Angel Spread.

CARD TWO: Influencing Factors = Three of Pentacles
As a card of the professional, I always strive to be my best at both the conjuring arts and the intuitive arts.

CARD THREE: Hopes = The Hierophant
This is a card of the teacher. I enjoy teaching classes on Tarot and other modalities. There is always something new to learn and discover.

CARD FOUR: Recent Past = Two of Swords Reversed
During the time I built this spread, I made some important life decisions, such as resigning from a job I was very unhappy with. This is the same card that shows up in my Angel Spread.

CARD FIVE: Distant Past = The Devil Reversed
Referring back to sobriety, it was Archangel Uriel, associated with The Devil Tarot card, that inspired me to take off those chains that bind.

CARD SIX: Future Influences = Two of Pentacles
This card represents living within my means and not getting into debt. This is the same card that shows up in my Angel Spread.

CARD SEVEN: Fears = Death Reversed
During this time, I wanted my projects to develop sooner. In recent years, these same projects are falling into place.

CARD EIGHT: Environmental Factors = King of Cups
This is how I always try to present myself. The King of Cups represents mastery over the realms of emotion, creativity, and the subconscious.

CARD NINE: Inner Emotions = Strength
The number eight is my life path number. The infinity sign (lemniscate) that appears above the woman's head is also the same one that appears above The Magician. It represents a balance of spiritual and carnal nature. This is the same card that shows up in my Angel Spread reversed.

CARD TEN: Possible Final Outcome = The High Priestess
The High Priestess represents a storehouse of spiritual knowledge sought through effort and hard work. These are the qualities that make me a better person. This is the same card that shows up in my Angel Spread.

CARD ELEVEN: Clarifier Card = Ace of Cups
I always approach life with love. I believe that whatever energy I send out, be it positive or negative, will be returned three times greater.

CARD TWELVE: Shadow Card = Two of Cups
Keeping the lines of communication open with the people in my life both professionally and personally. Being with like-minded people.

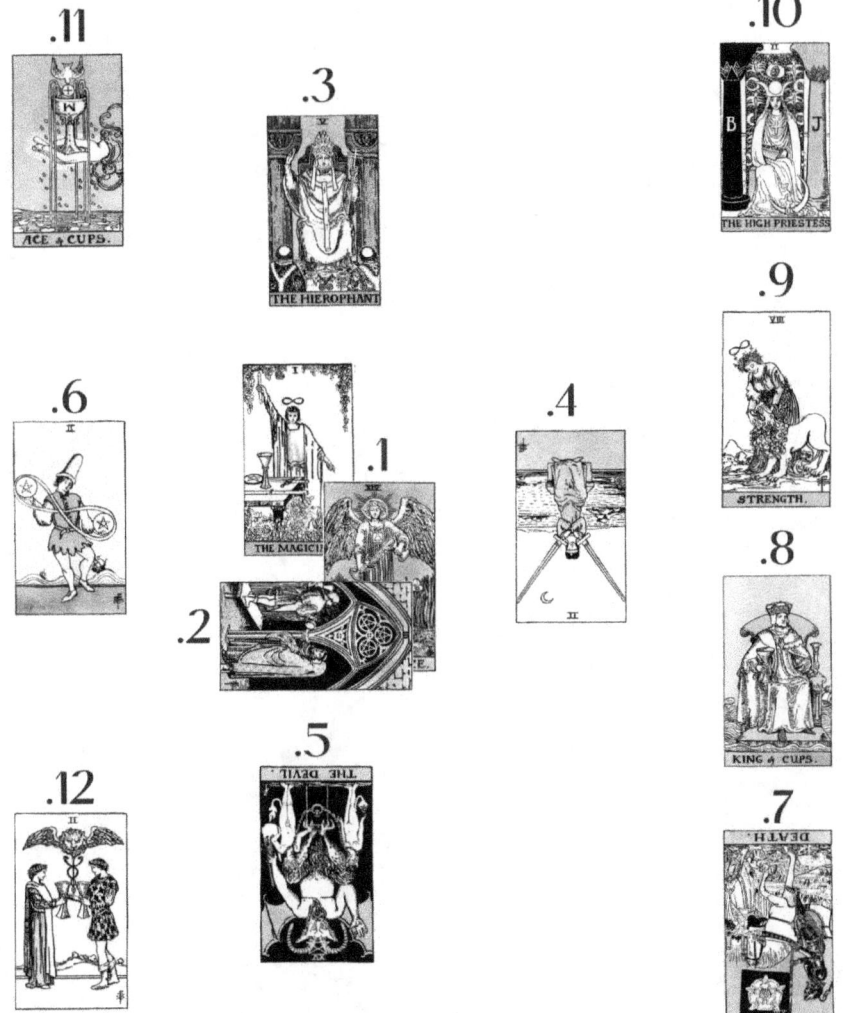

CHAPTER 4
Reading Playing Cards Tarot Style

As mentioned in the introduction, I've always been fascinated with sleight of hand magic. Before the advent of magic videos and YouTube, books were the main source of instruction.

During the late seventies, I was fortunate to have a magic teacher. We would get together every Saturday afternoon at The Fun Shop and session. I learned many excellent card and coin effects of the time. Playing cards have always had a long-standing influence on my life.

Over the years, I've read several books on cartomancy, but I wasn't happy with the definitions they provided. In 2018, I associated the basic meaning of Tarot with a regular deck of playing cards, which combine my two passions.

One of the features of playing cards is that they correspond to a calendar.

Two colors (red and black) symbolize day and night.

Four suites correspond to the four seasons.

Twelve court cards correspond to the twelve months in a year.

Thirteen values of cards ranging from Ace through King correspond to the thirteen lunar cycles.

When you add up all the values of a suit, starting with Ace as one through to King as thirteen, you get a total of ninety-one: the number of days in a season.

When you multiply 91x4, you get 364. When you add a joker, you get 365, the number of days in a year.

And if you add one more joker, you get 366, the number of days in a leap year. Because of these amazing correspondences, playing cards make an excellent tool for cartomancy!

Speaking of YouTube, check out my channel under Alan Dee Geddes for some of my favorite card and coin routines, as well as original effects and handlings.

The Anatomy of Tarot as Applied to Playing Cards
Based upon my observations of the artwork in the Waite-Smith deck, I have selected cards that have similar energy between the Major and Minor Arcana. In turn, I've layered these meanings onto the fifty-three cards of a regular deck.

To illustrate my point of view in cups, the image of the Two of Cups (hearts) complements The Lovers. The image of the Eight of Cups (hearts) complements The Moon because of the eclipse illustrated on the card. The image of the cloaked man in the Five of Cups (hearts) complements The Tower.

An almost equal number of suits have been distributed in the mix. I feel that six spade cards (one extra) are appropriate because swords represent the element of air, which is connected to thought. Thought is connected to spirit.

My selection of cards

The Joker

Four Aces

Three Twos: Hearts, Spades, and Clubs

Two Fours: Spades and Clubs

Two Fives: Diamonds and Hearts

Three Sixes: Clubs, Spades, and Diamonds

One Eight: Hearts

Two Nines: Spades and Hearts

Two Tens: Clubs and Diamonds

One Queen: Diamonds

One King: Spades

Suit Distribution

Clubs / Wands – Five

Hearts / Cups – Five

Spades / Swords – Six

Diamonds / Pentacles – Five

Because my selection process is based upon the artwork of the Minor Arcana, here are the cards that are not listed in the memory aid:

One Two: Diamonds

All Four Threes

Two Fours: Diamonds and Hearts

Two Fives: Spades and Clubs

One Six: Hearts

All Four Sevens

Three Eights: Clubs, Spades, and Diamonds

Two Nines: Clubs and Diamonds

Two Tens: Spades and Hearts

All Four Jacks
Three Queens: Spades, Clubs, and Hearts
Three Kings: Clubs, Hearts, and Diamonds

These card definitions can be found in Chapter 12: Discovering the Arcana. Remember to substitute clubs for wands, hearts for cups, spades for swords, and diamonds for pentacles. Jacks represent Pages. Knights are not included in the mix because they galloped away. (Small joke.)

Memory Aid

0 - JOKER - The Fool – beginnings, optimism, freedom

1 - ACE OF DIAMONDS - The Magician – astonishment, cleverness, manifestation

2 - ACE OF SPADES - The High Priestess – intuition, gut feelings, sacred knowledge

3 - QUEEN OF DIAMONDS - The Empress - abundance, nurturing, fertility

4 - KING OF SPADES - The Emperor – potency, ambition, structure

5 - FIVE OF DIAMONDS - The Hierophant – tradition, religion, hierarchy

6 - TWO OF HEARTS - The Lovers – sexuality, choice, healing

7 - SIX OF CLUBS - The Chariot – balance, willpower, determination

8 - ACE OF CLUBS - Strength – courage, fortitude, passion

9 - SIX OF SPADES - The Hermit - meditation, solitude, consciousness

10 - SIX OF DIAMONDS - Wheel of Fortune - cycles, change, ups and downs

11 - TWO OF SPADES - Justice – equality, impartiality, morality

12 - TWO OF CLUBS - The Hanged Man – perspective, surrender, forgiveness

13 - FOUR OF SPADES - Death – transformation, ending, letting go

14 - ACE OF HEARTS - Temperance - balance, harmonizing, moderation

15 - NINE OF SPADES - The Devil – addiction, temptation, illusion

16 - FIVE OF HEARTS - The Tower – destruction, catastrophe, sudden insight

17 - NINE OF HEARTS - The Star – meditation, healing, wishes fulfilled

18 - EIGHT OF HEARTS - The Moon – intuition, reflection, mystery

19 - FOUR OF CLUBS - The Sun – knowing, illumination, happiness

20 - TEN OF CLUBS - Judgment - rebirth, a new phase, inner calling

21 - TEN OF DIAMONDS - The World - completion, wholeness, attainment

The Whole Enchilada Spread

This is an ideal spread to cast when using playing cards. It's easy to read and covers all the bases.

Shuffle and cut the deck using your favorite method.

Starting at the top row, from left to right, deal the first card representing the past; deal the second card representing the present; and deal the third card representing the future. Then below these three cards, starting at the left, deal the fourth card representing the body; deal the fifth card representing the mind; and deal the sixth card representing the spirit.

Proceed with the reading.

Clarifier cards and reverse card meanings can also be used.

Magic of the Nineteen Cards

Although this is a book of Tarot, I wanted to share with you one of my favorite self-working card effects based upon mathematics, just for fun. Give it a try!

First of all, you must use a full deck of fifty-two cards. Discard the Jokers and any advertising cards that usually come with a new deck.

I suggest you get a deck of cards and follow along with me.

Shuffle the cards as much as you would like. They can be in any order.

Holding the deck face down in your left hand, deal the top card face up. If this card is a ten or a face card, put it face down, starting a discard pile.

Assuming this top card is a six: Deal a card face up on top of it (seven), deal another card face up on top of that one (eight) deal another card face up on top of that one (nine), and finally, deal one last card face up on top of that one (ten), to complete the first pile.

Another example, assuming this top card is a four: Deal a card face up on top of it (five), deal another card face up on top of that one (six), deal another card face up on top of that one (seven), deal another card face up on top of that one (eight), deal another card face up on top of that one (nine), and finally, deal one last card face up on top of that one (ten), to complete the first pile.

When starting another pile, remember, if the top card is a ten or face card, set it on the discard pile face down.

Aces represent the number one.

Continue to build piles following this same procedure.

If you don't have enough cards to make a final pile, place these cards face down on the discard pile.

You should be left with approximately seven or eight face-up piles, each making up the sum of ten.

Now turn any three of these face-up piles face down. Place the rest of the remaining face-up piles face down on the discard pile. You will be left with three face-down piles.

Gather up the discard pile and hold it face down in your left hand. Deal nineteen cards face down on the table. (Magic of the Nineteen Cards!)

Turn over the top card of any of the two piles of the three. Add the value of these two cards together. For example, if you have a five and an eight, the total is thirteen.

With the deck still in your left hand, deal thirteen cards face down onto the nineteen cards.

Count the remaining cards you have in your hand. Let's say you have eight.

Turn over the top card of the face-down pile you haven't touched, and it will be an eight!

This effect works every time. Don't ask me how it's done, because I don't know. It's the magic of mathematics!

Magician John Mendoza made this routine popular through his teaching DVD titled *My Best (Volume 3)*, published in 2006.

CHAPTER 5
The Witches' Star Spread

In the winter of 1997, I wrote an article called "The Witches' Star Spread" for *MoonRise News*, a quarterly pagan magazine I helped publish when I worked at Kinko's in Salt Lake City, Utah. Here is my updated version.

This spread is based upon a variety of correspondences, including information from the Hermetic Order of the Golden Dawn. It's designed to be read on an altar cloth with a pentacle pattern. If you don't have an altar cloth, you can visualize a pentacle as you cast the spread.

To begin, shuffle and cut the deck using your favorite method.

By either utilizing an altar cloth or imagining a pentagram, deal the first card to Position One: earth. Deal the second card to Position Two: water. Deal the third card to Position Three: air. Deal the fourth card to Position Four: fire. Deal the fifth card to Position Five: spirit, to finish the spread. See the illustration at the end of this chapter.

Starting at Position One, proceed with the reading.

Clarifier cards and reverse card meanings can also be used.

A Ritual to Invoke A Pentacle
I make a ritual out of casting the spread. Here's how. Starting at the top point of the pentagram, the first-card position is dealt and moved to the bottom-left point; the second-card position is dealt and moved to the

upper-right point; the third-card position is dealt and moved to the upper-left point; the fourth-card position is dealt and moved to the bottom-right point; and finally, the fifth-card position is dealt and moved up to the top point. Still at the top point, going clockwise, move your hand around the pentagram. By following this procedure, you have invoked a pentacle. This will provide balance and protection to the spread.

Position One: Environmental Foundations – Earth

Suit Correspondence: Pentacles
Key Term: The Body, Matter
Moon Phase: New Moon
Direction: North
Season: Winter
Sense: Touch
Color: Green
Archangel: Uriel

Positive aspects: comfort, prosperity, success, recognition, winning.
Negative aspects: insecurity, discontent, greed, carelessness, manipulation.

Position Two: Emotional Foundations – Water

Suit Correspondence: Cups
Key Term: The Soul
Moon Phase: Waning Moon
Direction: West
Season: Autumn
Sense: Taste
Color: Blue
Archangel: Gabriel

Positive aspects: love, art, peace, health, ecstasy.
Negative aspects: rejection, loneliness, depression, sadness, intemperance.

Position Three: Intellectual Foundations – Air
Suit Correspondence: Swords
Key Term: The Mind
Moon Phase: Waxing Moon
Direction: East
Season: Spring
Sense: Smell
Color: Yellow
Archangel: Raphael

Positive aspects: enlightenment, determination, discipline, justice, courage.
Negative aspects: confusion, illusions, victimization, destructiveness, chaos.

Position Four: Motivational Foundations – Fire
Suit Correspondence: Wands
Key Term: The Will
Moon Phase: Full Moon
Direction: South
Season: Summer
Sense: Sight
Color: Red
Archangel: Michael

Positive aspects: fertility, invention, drive, confidence, optimism.
Negative aspects: impotence, difficulty, frustration, ineffectiveness, delays.

Position Five: Course of Action – Spirit
Major Arcana Correspondences: The Magician / The High Priestess
Season: The Turning Wheel
Direction: Center
Sense: Hearing
Color: Violet/White

The element of spirit does not have correspondences like the physical elements. Spirit is a bridge between the physical and the spiritual.

To Banish the Pentacle

If you would like to banish the pentacle at the end of the reading, start at the top point going counterclockwise and draw a circle around it. After that, gather the cards in reverse numerical order to release the energy of the spread into the universe.

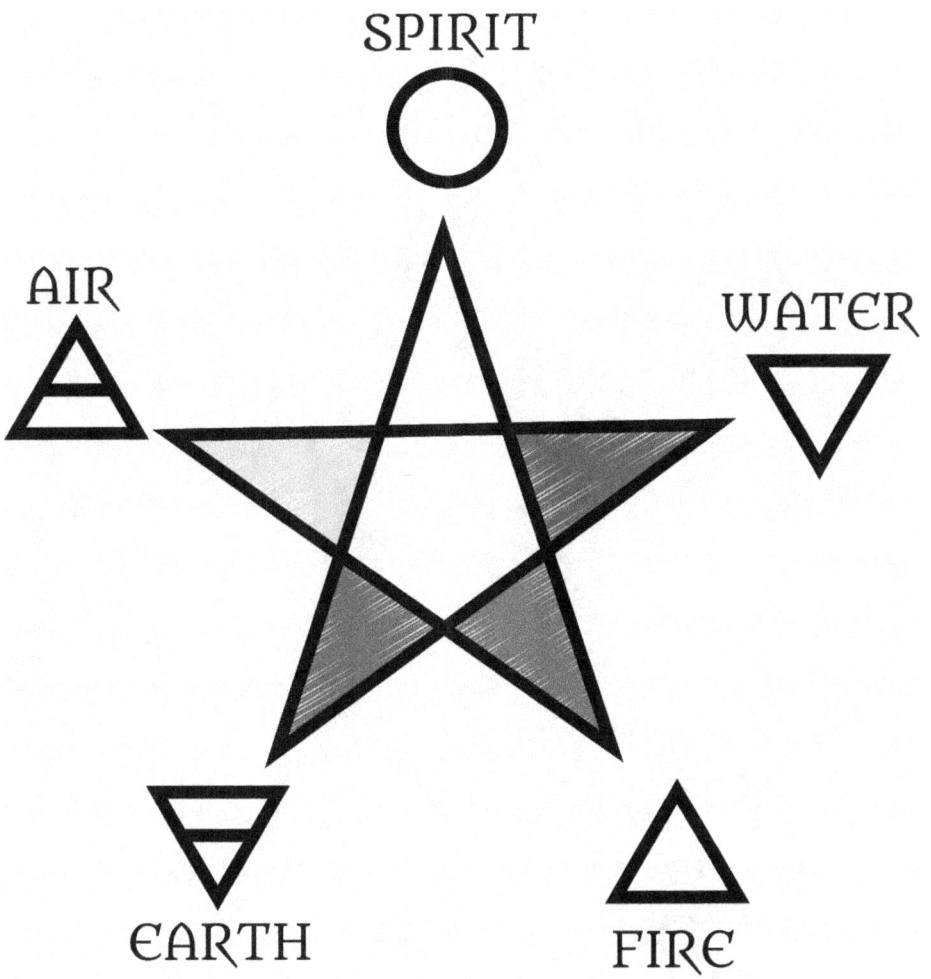

CHAPTER 6
Twelve-Step Tarot

After investigating Alcoholics Anonymous, it led me to think about which Major Arcana Tarot card would best match each of the Twelve Steps. In 1996, I published an essay on the subject. This book would not be complete without it.

Bill Wilson elaborated on the Six Steps of the Oxford Group (circa 1931) to form the Twelve Steps of Alcoholics Anonymous, published in 1939.

I believe that no one is ever "powerless." We all have free will to change!

As an alternative, I will be using the Empowerment Twelve Steps credited to Rev. Selena Fox, founder of Circle Sanctuary Nature Spirituality Church. She has graciously given me permission to include them here. Visit circlesanctuary.org for more information.

Step 1- We have recognized that we have given away personal power by addiction to substances or behaviors, that this has resulted in dysfunctional living, and that it is time to begin reclaiming our power and restoring balance to ourselves and our lives.
Tarot Card: The Devil - Self-imposed Limitations

Step 2 – Came to acknowledge that the Divine Power within can bring about healing change and harmony.
Tarot Card: The High Priestess - Intuitive Awareness

Step 3 - Chose to allow the Divine Power within of our own spiritual path to be the central guiding force in ourselves and our lives.
Tarot Card: The Fool - Beginning of a Journey

Step 4 - Examined ourselves deeply and honestly on all dimensions: physical, mental, behavioral, emotional, and spiritual.
Tarot Card: The Hermit - Searching Within

Step 5 - Acknowledged to the Divine, to our egos, and to at least one ally what is healthy and what is unhealthy and unbalanced in our bodies, thoughts, emotions, behaviors, and souls.
Tarot Card: The Hanged Man - A New Perspective

Step 6 - Were ready for the Divine within to work transformation to restore balance to ourselves and our lives.
Tarot Card: Strength - Moral Force

Step 7 - Sincerely invited the Divine within to dispel barriers to change and facilitate transformation.
Tarot Card: Death - Major Transformation

Step 8 – Made a list of all beings we have harmed, and became willing to make amends to them all.
Tarot Card: Judgment - Awakening of Personal Consciousness

Step 9 - Made direct amends to such beings as much as possible, except when to do so would cause harm to them or others or make a difficult situation worse.
Tarot Card: Justice - Karma

Step 10 – Continued our process of self-examination, acknowledging our strengths as well as our problems, and promptly acknowledging our

mistakes and our successes when they occurred.
Tarot Card: The Magician - Mastery of Special Knowledge

Step 11 - Sought through spiritual activities to strengthen our relationship with the Divine within and to allow this transpersonal dimension of ourselves to be the guiding force in our lives.
Tarot Card: The Star - Meditation

Step 12 - Having had a spiritual rebirth as a result of this process of healing transformation, we continue our work with these principles and are willing to share our story with those who come to us in need.
Tarot Card: Temperance - Balance

Serenity Prayer Spread

As a three-card spread, select one of the twelve-step cards you want to focus on and shuffle it into the deck. When finished, spread the cards face up until you find the twelve-step card. Remove it, as well as the two cards beneath, in order, and place them on the table.

The card on the left represents the first part of the prayer: "God, grant me the serenity to accept the things I cannot change" (situation). The energy of this card can reflect accepting life on life's terms. Acknowledging what we can and cannot change.

The card in the center represents the middle part of the prayer: "…the courage to change the things I can" (action). The energy of this card can reflect the courage of addressing a situation or problem. Tapping into inner strength.

The card on the right, the twelve-step card, represents the end part of the prayer: "…and wisdom to know the difference" (outcome). The energy of this card can reflect the wisdom you have in solving a situation or problem. Knowing when to stay or walk away.

CHAPTER 7
Etheric Cord Cutting
and the Sword Cards

After becoming a Reiki Master and incorporating etheric cord cutting into my practice, it inspired me to apply this modality to the Tarot. The Minor Arcana of the fourteen sword cards, in reverse, can tell a story about what kind of negative etheric cord exists, and how it can be cut. Here are my thoughts on how I incorporate this concept into each card.

I include my associations of the Major Arcana cards to the seven chakras where etheric cord cutting is applied. You will also find the twelve steps of etheric cord cutting, which describe in detail my technique for releasing unbalanced energy as part of a Reiki session.

Ace of Swords in Reverse
When this card shows up in a reading, it suggests that an etheric cord cutting may be needed, based on the surrounding cards. The Ace of Swords can also be used as a tool for etheric cord cutting.

Two of Swords in Reverse
Two equally important points of view that can represent a stalemate. By cutting the etheric cord, I visualize the blindfold coming off so that clarity of vision can be used to choose the appropriate sword.

Three of Swords in Reverse
As the etheric cord is being cut, I visualize each sword dropping away. The remaining symbolic scars can represent life lessons that provide a more stable emotional foundation.

Four of Swords in Reverse
This card represents the acknowledgment of laying down our sword by cutting the etheric cord, enabling us to take a mental break.

Five of Swords in Reverse
By cutting the etheric cord, I envision becoming free of hollow victories, one-upmanship, and being independent of the "good" opinion of others.

Six of Swords in Reverse
I visualize the wavy water at the top holding us back. By cutting the etheric cord, we are able to move forward to smoother sailing.

Seven of Swords in Reverse
This card represents someone or something negative living in our heads rent-free. I visualize the etheric cord being cut to take back our mental energy.

Eight of Swords in Reverse
This is a card that reflects feeling stuck even though we are free to walk away. As the etheric cord is being cut, I visualize the blindfold and binding coming off, providing new freedom to move forward.

Nine of Swords in Reverse
This card illustrates a disturbance in our sleeping patterns. By cutting the etheric cord, negative energy is released to achieve restful sleep.

Ten of Swords in Reverse
This represents the ultimate energy of the suit. As the etheric cord is being cut, I visualize each sword dropping away, opening up channels for a new cycle.

Court Cards in Reverse
Court cards represent people in our life we attach negative etheric cords to. Bakara Wintner personalizes these cards by associating them with daughter (Page), son (Knight), mother (Queen), and father (King). Focusing on the appropriate court card representing this person can be an effective tool to cut the etheric cord in an unhealthy relationship.

Chakra and Tarot Associations

Crown: Color – violet/white
The Fool, The Magician, The High Priestess

Third Eye: Color – indigo
The Star, The Moon, The Hanged Man

Throat: Color – blue
The Hierophant, The Hermit, Wheel of Fortune

Heart: Color – green
The Lovers, Temperance, The Sun

Solar Plexus: Color – yellow
Justice, Strength, The Chariot

Sacral: Color – orange
The Empress, The Emperor, The Devil, The Tower

Root: Color – red
The World, Death, Judgment

Twelve Steps of Etheric Cord Cutting

1 - Create a sacred space. In a quiet, comfortable room, smudge to clear the area. Burn your favorite incense. Apply the cleansing techniques you are most comfortable with.

2 - Ground and center. Close your eyes. Take in and release three deep breaths.

3 - Identify the negative etheric cords that need to be removed. Think about how this person, place, or thing has negatively affected your life.

4 - Review the lessons you have learned. What are the life lessons you have learned from these negative etheric cords that make you a more authentic person?

5 - Call in your Higher Power, including your archangels and spirit guides.

6 - Activate the chakras. Starting at the Root, move your hands over your body to scan each chakra, ending with the Crown to determine which of the seven are affected.

7 - Ask yourself permission to remove these negative etheric cords, as it is going to require dedicated work.

8 - Remove the negative etheric cords. In a downward pulling gesture, visualize these negative etheric cords being removed from each chakra, starting at the Root and ending at the Crown.

9 - Replace the negative etheric cords with positive energy. Imagine a brilliant white light cleansing each chakra immediately after these negative etheric cords have been removed.

10 - Balance all chakras. Still at the Crown, visualize any unbalanced energy being removed by a downward pulling gesture as you continue through each chakra, ending at the Root. From there, send all unbalanced energy down to Mother Earth.

11 - Thank your Higher Power, archangels, and spirit guides for being present in this process. It is through their divine influence that only positive etheric cords remain.

12 - Complete homework. Write down how these negative etheric cords have affected your life and the lessons you have learned. During a full moon, burn your words to release this energy into the universe.

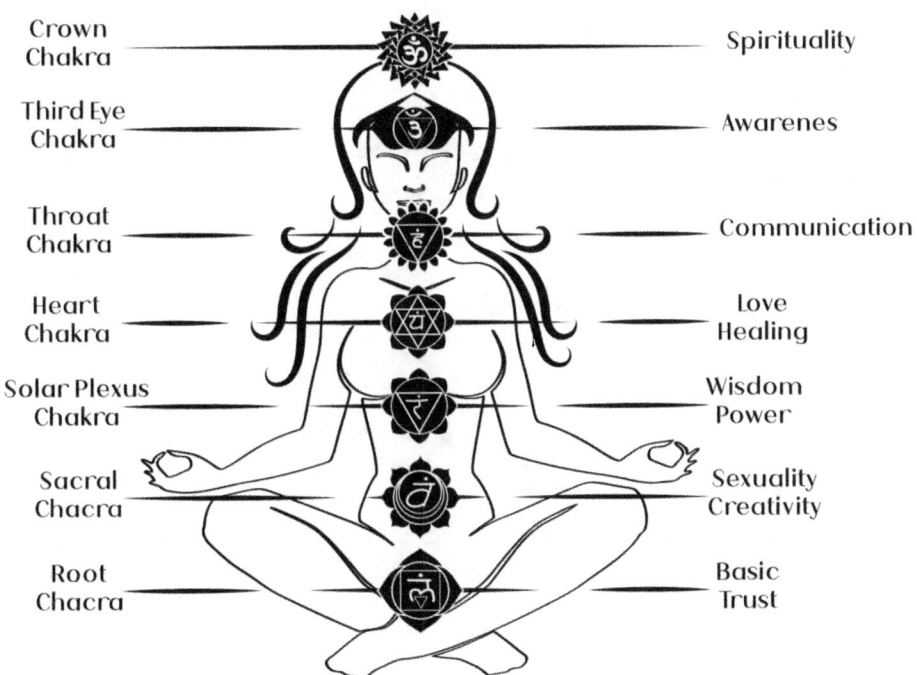

Crown Chakra — Spirituality

Third Eye Chakra — Awarenes

Throat Chakra — Communication

Heart Chakra — Love Healing

Solar Plexus Chakra — Wisdom Power

Sacral Chacra — Sexuality Creativity

Root Chacra — Basic Trust

CHAPTER 8
The Moon and Tarot

The eight phases of the moon can be connected to the Major Arcana. Understanding and meditating on the meaning of the cards associated with each lunar phase will help you connect with the present moment and realize the possibilities available to you. When you align your life with the phases of the moon and the intuitive messages of the Tarot, you will find greater ease, deeper meaning, and more potential in your life. Since gazing at the moon is an outside activity, I've also included my associations of the eight Sabbats to the Major Arcana.

The New Moon Phase – The Star
During a New Moon, stars are brought into focus. It is a time for wishes, new ideas, and new projects. To quote Neville Goddard: "Feel the feeling of the wish fulfilled. Feel it in your body. Feel the elation. Feel it in the now."

The Waxing Crescent Moon Phase – The High Priestess
As the fingernail of the Waxing Crescent Moon starts to appear, so do your intuitive abilities. Use this time to discover your gifts through the influence of the High Priestess.

The First Quarter Moon Phase – The Magician
The Magician manipulates the four elements on his table to manifest spirit into reality. The First Quarter Moon can represent "As Above, So Below," as well as Yin and Yang.

The Waxing Gibbous Moon Phase – The Empress

The Waxing Gibbous Moon gives us fertility of the Empress, bringing into fruition all we have created from the previous two phases.

The Full Moon Phase – The Moon

Because of the heightened energy of the Full Moon, we are in touch with our emotions on a deeper level. This is the time to release any unbalanced energy.

The Waning Gibbous Moon Phase – Temperance

Through the release of the Waning Gibbous Moon, Temperance is the result of finding balance and equilibrium. The presence of Archangel Michael is here to protect and assist us.

The Last Quarter Moon Phase – Judgment

Having obtained balance, as reflected by the Last Quarter Moon, we are able to hear the clarion call of Archangel Gabriel directing us to share the "music" (life calling) that lies within.

The Waning Crescent Moon Phase – The Hermit

As the energy dissipates, we retreat to the Waning Crescent Moon. The Hermit signifies the need to reflect and heal in readiness for the next lunar cycle.

Sabbats and the Major Arcana

Samhain, All Hallows' Eve: (October 31 - November 1)
the end harvest ~ remembering our ancestors ~ the thinning veil
The Fool, Death

Yule, Winter Solstice: (December 19 - 23)
rebirth ~ return of light ~ heralding promise
The Magician, The High Priestess

Imbolc, Candlemas: (February 1 - 2)
creativity ~ the Goddess ~ new beginnings
The Hierophant, The Hermit, The Star

Ostara, Spring Equinox: (March 19 - 23)
balance ~ renewal ~ rebirth
The Empress, The Hanged Man, Temperance

Beltane, May Day: (April 30 - May 1)
fertility ~ union ~ honoring the earth
The Lovers, The Devil, The Tower

Litha, Summer Solstice: (June 19 - 23)
abundance ~ culmination ~ nature's bounty
The Sun, Strength, The Emperor

Lammas, Lughnasad: (August 1 - 2)
the first harvest ~ baking bread ~ leaving offerings
The Moon, The Chariot, Justice

Mabon, Fall Equinox: (September 20 - 23)
the second harvest ~ thanksgiving ~ gratitude
The World, Wheel of Fortune, Judgment.

Moon Phases

last quarter

waning crescent

waning gibbous

new moon

full moon

waxing crescent

waxing gibbous

first quarter

CHAPTER 9
The Archangels of Tarot

The date was Saturday, June 10, 2017. That afternoon, I attended an open circle at a new-age shop in Ogden, Utah. The topic was spirit guides. We discussed the many forms they take, including guardian angels.

That following Sunday morning, I consulted the cards for a reading. I asked about the spirit guides in my life, and three archangels appeared! The surrounding cards were also right on target. Because this spread had such an impact, I took a picture of it with my smartphone. You will find the interpretation at the end of this chapter.

What follows is a collection of interpretations, associations, and observations, including those from the Hermetic Order of the Golden Dawn.

The Lovers – Archangel Raphael
"God's Healing"
Suit – Swords
Element – Air
Color - Yellow
Direction – East
Season – Spring
Zodiac Signs – Gemini, Libra, Aquarius

When Archangel Raphael appears, his basic energy represents healing. He presides over the superconscious. Here, we learn that the three levels of the mind are not separate and isolated but that the superconscious is actually a product of the subconscious and conscious joined together where we find the true energy of life.

On The Lovers card, the man looks at the woman, who looks at the archangel, symbolizing the balance between physical desire and spiritual needs. Also, the man and woman represent important choices between the two. On the left is the tree of knowledge, and on the right is the tree of life. The sun above represents passionate healing energy. Archangel Raphael illuminates our lives on all levels.

Temperance – Archangel Michael
"Like unto God"
Suit – Wands
Element – Fire
Color - Red
Direction – South
Season – Summer
Zodiac Signs – Aries, Leo, Sagittarius

When Archangel Michael appears, his basic energy represents protection. Often represented with his flaming blue sword, he cuts through negative etheric cords that no longer serve us. As a result, this releases all unbalanced energy, fears, limiting beliefs, and negative energetic imprints.

On the Temperance card, the archangel is shown mixing water from two chalices, presumably one hot and the other cold to get the perfect mix. This signifies balance and harmony in our lives. He stands with one foot on land and one foot in water, symbolizing the connection between the subconscious and consciousness.

Judgment - Archangel Gabriel

"God's Might"
Suit - Cups
Element - Water
Color - Blue
Direction - West
Season - Autumn
Zodiac Signs - Cancer, Scorpio, Pisces

When Archangel Gabriel appears, she represents the clarion call, a transformation and upliftment in our lives. The realization of our life purpose in this current incarnation. Dancing to our own tune. Sharing the "music" (life calling) that resides within.

On the Judgment card, the archangel is blowing her horn to the tune of a new awareness, a transformation, and an inspiration. The people rising out of the coffins represent deliverance. Newfound freedom. Not feeling boxed in anymore. Thinking outside the box.

The Devil - Archangel Uriel

"God's Light"
Suit - Pentacles
Element - Earth
Color - Green
Direction - North
Season - Winter
Zodiac Signs: Taurus, Virgo, Capricorn

When Archangel Uriel appears, his basic energy represents enlightenment. He exposes enslavement to earthly or material forms of desire. These could be external or self-imposed. He asks us to release these attachments in order to free ourselves from limitations and oppression.

On the Devil card, the chains around the necks of the couple are loose. They could take them off if they wanted to. In that sense, this is a card of hope. There may be a reluctance or refusal to leave an unhealthy situation or dependency. Occasionally, however, this is an invitation to break loose, and have a devil-may-care attitude!

The Wheel of Fortune and The World
Raphael - upper left
Uriel - lower left
Gabriel - upper right
Michael - lower right

When the Wheel of Fortune or The World card appears, its basic message represents an acknowledgment of all four archangels of the Tarot. Either in the earthly plane as represented by the Wheel of Fortune, or the spiritual plane as represented by The World.

There are times in our lives when the archangels are wanting our attention to give us guidance and support. This is never more evident than when they appear in readings. Sometimes, they drop in just to show us they are with us and to remind us that all we have to do is ask for their help.

My Angel Spread and Interpretation

Significator Card: Two of Swords

I prefer to have the significator card find itself, as mentioned in Chapter 2: The Celtic Cross Spread. I was contemplating important decisions in my life. This is the same card that shows up in my Vision Spread reversed.

CARD ONE: Present Situation = King of Swords

During that time, I was studying the metaphysical and conjuring arts, which require a lot of memorization.

CARD TWO: Influencing Factors = Ace of Wands reversed

The Ace of Wands can represent a magic wand as well as a paintbrush. It was an acknowledgment that these two energies were going to play an important part in my life.

CARD THREE: Hopes = Strength reversed

A message to continue to take care of my physical health. This is the same card that shows up in my Vision Spread.

CARD FOUR: Recent Past = Temperance (Archangel Michael)

Archangel Michael is always present in my life. This is the same card that shows up in my Vision Spread.

CARD FIVE: Distant Past = Two of Pentacles

Another reminder to live within my means and not get into debt. This is the same card that shows up in my Vision Spread.

CARD SIX: Future Influences = Judgment (Archangel Gabriel)

The Judgment card represents the clarion call to share the "music" (life calling) we all have in our own unique way.

CARD SEVEN: Fears = Five of Swords Reversed

An important message to not sweat the small stuff like hollow victories and one-upmanship. Life is too short.

CARD EIGHT: Environmental Factors = Knight of Pentacles

In the Knight of Pentacles, the horse is stationary. This represents a dedication to the projects I am involved with.

CARD NINE: Inner Emotions = The Lovers (Archangel Raphael)

Having love for all beings. It also represents self-love. Making the right choices. The balance between physical desire and spiritual needs.

CARD TEN: Possible Final Outcome = The High Priestess

The High Priestess represents a storehouse of spiritual knowledge sought through effort and hard work. These are the qualities that make me a better person. This is the same card that shows up in my Vision Spread.

CARD ELEVEN: Clarifier Card = Five of Cups

Even though there have been emotional losses in the past, I always acknowledge the two cups that remain standing.

CARD TWELVE: Shadow Card = Eight of Cups

This card reflects my desire to go back to the activities I loved when I was younger, and develop these talents to a further degree.

The absence of Archangel Uriel:

The reason why I believe Archangel Uriel didn't show up in this spread is that I have already incorporated his healing energy into my life.

CHAPTER 10
The Horses of Tarot

There are seven horses portrayed in the Waite-Smith deck:

Knight of Wands
Knight of Pentacles
Knight of Swords
Knight of Cups
Six of Wands
The Sun
Death

Horse meanings include determination, endurance, freedom, majesty, and spirit.

Visualizing the Celtic Cross Spread as a map, these horses will travel from card to card. They can represent moving forward, moving away, being stationary, or slowing down, as represented by the Knight of Swords in reverse. Equestrian movements include two horses that are traveling to the left, and four traveling to the right. One is stationary.

The horse in The Sun Tarot card is the only one that does not have reins. (Freedom.)

Color of Horses
Knight of Wands- brown
Knight of Pentacles- black

Knight of Swords- gray
Knight of Cups- gray
Six of Wands- gray
The Sun- white
Death- white

Color Significance
Brown- stability, wholesomeness, nature
Black- mystery, protection, transition
Gray- security, reliability, intelligence
White- innocence, illumination, perfection

Numerical Significance
12 - Knights: inspiration, exploration, interpretation
6 - Six of Wands: harmony, contentment, alignment
19 - The Sun: beginnings and endings, enthusiasm, happiness
13 - Death: metaphysical, groundwork, transformation

To make this chapter complete, I've included a section for those who own a Tarot deck that has horses portrayed in the Chariot card instead of the two sphinxes, as illustrated in the Waite-Smith deck.

Horses (and sphinxes) represent a union of opposites: one black horse and one white horse. They can express that even if opposites try to pull in different directions, they need to be channeled in the same direction if progress is to be made.

This reflects the desire to achieve control over opposing emotions, circumstances, motivations, and challenges. A sense of determination. A successful balance of the necessary forces. An advancement in self-actualization and development.

More Keywords

Independence
Self-sufficiency
Fortitude
Harnessing
Work
Travel
Purpose
Triumph

CHAPTER 11
Numerology and Tarot

I would be remiss if I didn't include a section on numerology since my daughter, Alasun Geddes, is an expert in this field. With her encouragement and contributions, here is a list of keywords for the numbers zero through twenty-one.

Tarot court cards don't have numerical associations, however, in a standard deck of playing cards, face cards are numbered eleven for Jacks, twelve for Queens, and thirteen for Kings. If you apply this same logic to the court cards of the Tarot, Pages become eleven, Knights become twelve, Queens become thirteen, and Kings become fourteen.

Number 0: Wholeness, Inclusiveness, Possibilities, Potential, Boundlessness, Infinite

Number 1: Beginnings, Sparks, Inspiration, Capability, Opportunity, Individuality

Number 2: Duality, Choices, Balance, Union, Partnership, Collaboration

Number 3: Interaction, Communication, Expression, Creation, Development, Multiplication

Number 4: Foundations, Stability, Structure, Construction, Protection, Manifestation

Number 5: Conflict, Movement, Instability, Difficulties, Struggles, Resistance

Number 6: Harmony, Contentment, Adjustment, Cooperation, Alignment, Reconciliation

Number 7: Spirituality, Introspection, Understanding, Assessment, Reevaluation, Pondering

Number 8: Movement, Accomplishment, Speed, Achievement, Mastery, Alignment

Number 9: Attainment, Perfection, Transition, Wisdom, Idealism, Fruition

Number 10: Fulfillment, Culmination, Excess, Finality, Closure, Renewal

Number 11: Intuition, Charisma, Imagination, Spontaneity, Visualization, Magnetism

Number 12: Creativity, Friendship, Incentive, Exploration, Interpretation, Explanation

Number 13: Philosophy, Authority, Courage, Groundwork, Independence, Premonition

Number 14: Freedom, Determination, Strength, Experience, Persistence, Steadfastness

Number 15: Morality, Healing, Examination, Curiosity, Moderation, Consensus

Number 16: Boldness, Autonomy, Insight, Enthusiasm, Education, Contemplation

Number 17: Materialism, Business, Goals, Manifestations, Efficiency, Building

Number 18: Compassion, Benevolence, Dedication, Patience, Adaptability, Philanthropy

Number 19: Tolerance, Decisions, Resolution, Devotion, Initiative, Completion

Number 20: Relationships, Teamwork, Coexistence, Service, Companionship, Diplomacy

Number 21: Expression, Optimism, Reliability, Compromise, Association, Judgment

CHAPTER 12
Discovering the Arcana

Below are the images of the Waite-Smith deck, which was published in 1909 by Arthur Edward Waite and Pamela Colman Smith. Commonly known as the Rider-Waite, it is still the most popular Tarot deck for both beginner and professional card readers.

The Major Arcana

The Fool: Innocence, optimism, freedom, beginnings, spontaneity, a disembodied spirit, embarking on an exciting journey, gifts of past lives carried in the satchel.

Reversed: Apprehension, immaturity, gullibility, irresponsibility, foolish abandonment, being unprepared, holding back, risk-taking.

The Magician

Astonishment, cleverness, dexterity, manifestation, resourcefulness, "as above, so below," the superconscious and subconscious delivered to consciousness.

Reversed: Trickery, illusion, manipulation, indiscriminate, a charlatan, magical thinking, poor planning, untapped talents.

The High Priestess

Intuition, gut feelings, lunar consciousness, sacred knowledge, maiden, mother, crone, beneath the surface, hidden connection between spirit and material, the eternal feminine.

Reversed: Secrets, repression, inconstancy, superficial knowledge, ignoring one's intuition, withdrawal, and silence.

The Empress

Fertility, creativity, luxury, sensuality, Earth Mother, the passive, the nurturer, the subconscious, a fertile imagination, intuitive, over-analytical.

Reversed: Overindulgence, temptation, infertility, stagnation, withholding affection, creative block, co-dependence, not going with the flow.

The Emperor

Potency, majesty, ambition, structure, leadership, discipline, Earth Father, the aggressive, the provider, the conscious, analytical, over-intuitive.

Reversed: Domination, arrogance, vanity, tyranny, immaturity, inflexibility, ineffectiveness, abuse of power, lack of discipline.

The Hierophant

Tradition, religion, hierarchy, the teacher, ritual structure, the conventional, divine revelation, the eternal masculine.

Reversed: The non-traditional, exploring modalities such as Tarot, intuitive, and healing arts. Adversely: Intolerance, dogmatism, social pressure.

The Lovers

Discernment, attraction, harmony, enchantment, divine love, cupid's arrow, connection of the subconscious and consciousness, healing energy as directed through Archangel Raphael.

Reversed: Self-love. Adversely: Imbalance, incompatibility, disharmony, betrayal, misalignment of values, lack of commitment, troubled relationships.

The Chariot
Balance, willpower, determination, control, moving forward, letting your conscience be your guide, successful conclusion to the first phase (the practical plane) of The Fool's Journey.

Reversed: Opposition, distraction, fixation, apathetic, spinning wheels, lack of direction, backing out of a situation, possible car trouble or needed maintenance.

Strength
Courage, fortitude, passion, vitality, self-esteem, hidden strength, balance between spiritual and carnal nature, creating harmony amid opposing forces.

Reversed: Vulnerability, insecurity, low energy, self-doubt, lack of courage, abuse of power, carnal over spiritual, self will run riot.

The Hermit

Wisdom, meditation, prudence, discernment, soul-searching, self-awareness, seeking that which is illuminated in the glowing lantern, getting in touch with spirit through nature.

Reversed: Returning from seclusion, applying spiritual knowledge sought through meditation. Adversely: Disconnectedness, loneliness, social isolation, feeling lost.

Wheel of Fortune

Opportunities, lady luck, upward trend, decisive moments, life cycles, seasons and sabbats, angelic influences, applying the law of attraction.

Reversed: Missed opportunities, clinging to control, downward trend, breaking cycles, resistance to change, going around in circles.

Justice

Equality, impartiality, morality, law and order, contemplating the scales of balance, striving to be a better person today than what we were in the past.

Reversed: Karma, injustice, bias, dishonesty, corruption, unfair treatment, laws in our society that need to be changed.

The Hanged Man

Perspective, surrender, forgiveness, willingness to make a sacrifice for greater spiritual understanding, when you change the way you look at things, the things you look at change.

Reversed: Moving forward to apply the knowledge you have attained through self-sacrifice. Adversely: Inactivity, resistance, fear of sacrifice.

Death

Transformation, transition, metamorphosis, letting go, moving on, necessary mourning, out with the old, in with the new.

Reversed: Stagnation, procrastination, fear of change, refusing to let go, living in the past.

Temperance

Moderation, harmonizing, secrets of transforming spirit from the subconscious into the activity of consciousness, healing energy as directed through Archangel Michael, successful conclusion to the second phase (the mental plane) of The Fool's Journey.

Reversed: Immoderation, unbalanced energy, losing control, numbing our senses through the use of alcohol and/or hard drugs.

The Devil

Addiction, illusion, obsession, temptation, enslavement, repression, shadow self, religious fanaticism, and self-imposed restrictions.

Reversed: Reclaiming power, free will to change, casting off the chains that bind, adopting a spiritual perspective, healing energy as directed through Archangel Uriel.

The Tower

Destruction, collapse, disaster, catastrophe, upheaval, trauma.

Reversed: Personal transformation, sudden revelation, averting disaster, a powerful equalizing force, a radical change that brings enlightenment.

The Star

Meditation, tranquility, healing, wishes fulfilled, clarity of vision, balance of the seven chakras, insight, inspiration, and hope.

Reversed: Hopelessness, pessimism, disconnection, unbalanced chakras, be careful what you wish for because it might come true!

The Moon

Goddess energy, intuition, reflection, mystery, unseen influences, cycles of the moon, hidden behind the shadows.

Reversed: Something waning, psychic awareness, new revelations, sight beyond the shadows.

The Sun

God energy, knowing, illumination, happiness, freedom, moving forward, sunny disposition, a passion for life.

Reversed: The inner child, the same but to a lesser degree. Adversely: Unable to acknowledge the good because of feeling unworthy or having low self-esteem.

Judgment

Self-awareness, dancing to your own tune, the reawakening of nature under the influence of spirit, healing energy as directed through Archangel Gabriel.

Reversed: Indecisiveness, self-doubt, inner critic, don't die with the "music" (life calling) still inside you!

The World

Completion, achievement, fulfillment, wholeness, harmony, sense of being, successful conclusion to the final phase (the spiritual plane) of The Fool's Journey.

Reversed: Seeking personal closure.
Adversely: Delays, shortcuts, emptiness, feeling incomplete, lack of achievement.

The Minor Arcana

Ace of Wands - Fire
Inspiration, creativity, a paint brush, enthusiastic beginnings.

Reversed: Hesitation, impotence, creative blocks, lack of direction.

Two of Wands
Optimism, world view, future planning, choosing between adventure or security.

Reversed: Unbalance, hesitating to choose, lack of planning, fear of the unknown.

Three of Wands
Enterprise, productivity, momentum, networking.

Reversed: Your "ships" are coming in. Adversely: Disappointment, missed opportunities, unexpected delays.

Four of Wands

Stability, harmony, celebration, and family events such as picnics and weddings.

Reversed: Personal celebration, inner harmony. Adversely: Conflict with others, possible delay in plans.

Five of Wands

Tension, competition, chaotic energy, testing your mettle.

Reversed: Direct enthusiasm, conflict avoidance, focusing energy, a pentagram taking form representing completion.

Six of Wands

Victory, recognition, self-confidence, moving forward (as represented by the only horse in the Waite-Smith pip cards.)

Reversed: Independent of the crowd. Adversely: Vanity, fall from grace, lack of achievement.

Seven of Wands

Stamina, determination, challenges, a position of advantage.

Reversed: Choosing your battles. Adversely: Defensiveness, feeling attacked, self-victimization.

Eight of Wands

Alignment, a rapid series of events, positive movement, arrows of love.

Reversed: Coming in for a landing. A settling of energy. Adversely: Delays, arrows of jealousy.

Nine of Wands

Boundaries, determination, resilience, courage.

Reversed: Inner resources, alternate solutions. Adversely: Stubbornness, defensiveness.

Ten of Wands
Burden, overstretched, hard work, extra responsibility.

Reversed: Release, delegation. Adversely: Burnout, collapse.

Page of Wands - Earth of Fire
Enthusiastic, youthful energy, new perspectives, limitless potential.

Reversed: Distractions, wasted energy, false starts, lack of initiative.

Knight of Wands - Fire of Fire
Ambitious, adventuresome, moving forward, business travel.

Reversed: Unpredictability, impulsive, overbearing, possible setbacks.

Queen of Wands – Water of Fire

Creativity, extroverted, self-confidence, a fiery personality.

Reversed: Cattiness, impatience, jealousy, unfaithfulness.

King of Wands - Air of Fire

Tenacity, visionary leader, trial by fire, tendency to take charge.

Reversed: Domineering, arrogant, acting on impulse, difficult to manage.

Ace of Cups - Water

Love, healing, compassion, emotional support.

Reversed: Dissatisfaction, loneliness, repressed emotions, inadequate nourishment.

Two of Cups

Attraction, communication, partnerships, emotional bond.

Reversed: Self-love. Adversely: Incompatibility, disharmony, lack of communication.

Three of Cups

Friendship, collaboration, social circle, the party card.

Reversed: Selfishness, competitiveness, overindulgence, phony friends.

Four of Cups

Boredom, depression, indifference, not acknowledging the gift in front of you.

Reversed: Motivation, enthusiasm, awareness, accepting the gift in front of you.

Five of Cups

Sorrow, grief, disappointment, emotional loss.

Reversed: Forgiveness, recovery, moving on, acknowledging the two cups that remain standing.

Six of Cups

Nostalgia, innocence, childhood friendships, the good old days.

Reversed: Independence, moving forward, healing childhood pain, the good new days.

Seven of Cups

Distractions, daydreaming, overstimulation, and possible addictive behavior.

Reversed: Stepping back to look at the bigger picture, making a choice out of many possibilities, taking action on fantasies, telling people your desires and dreams.

Eight of Cups

Abandonment, withdrawal, moving on, seeking deeper meaning. (An effect of the full moon or eclipse often triggers these feelings.)

Reversed: A new perspective, lifestyle changes, trying one more time, revisiting and further developing activities that resonated in the past.

Nine of Cups

Pleasure, contentment, satisfaction, the wish card.

Reversed: "Hidden things revealed, virtues of truth and loyalty over personal satisfaction." - Arthur Edward Waite. Adversely: Materialism, overindulgence.

Ten of Cups

Happiness, harmony, family, alignment of chakras as represented by the rainbow.

Reversed: Dissatisfaction, domestic disputes, dysfunctional family, unbalanced chakras.

Page of Cups - Earth of Water

Inner child, adolescent love, psychic information, the birth of new ideas.

Reversed: Insecurity, emotional immaturity, creative blocks, doubting intuition.

Knight of Cups - Fire of Water

Passion, chivalrous, knight in shining armor, a relationship moving forward.

Reversed: A Don Juan, narcissistic, a one-night stand, moving away from responsibility.

Queen of Cups - Water of Water

Nurturing, creative, supportive, romantic love or love of family.

Reversed: Insecurity, depression, codependency, overly sensitive.

King of Cups - Air of Water
Compassionate, deep emotions, creative impulses, a professional artist.

Reversed: Anger, resentment, uncaring, possibly someone with a drinking problem.

Ace of Swords - Air
Ideas, keen insight, singleness of mind, clarity of thought.

Reversed: Confusion, conflict, hostility, stick a fork in it because it's done!

Two of Swords
Indecision, hesitation, uncertainty, stalemate.

Reversed: Balancing viewpoints, dropping defenses, the blindfold coming off, choosing the appropriate sword.

Three of Swords

Heartbreak, deep sadness, emotional upset, possible surgery.

Reversed: Forgiveness, reconciliation, healing of the heart, working through grief.

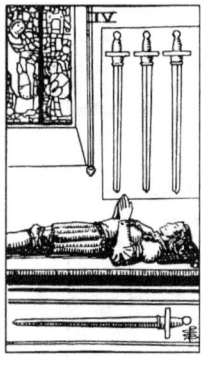

Four of Swords

Meditation, recuperation, sanctuary, inner peace.

Reversed: Contemplation, renewed energy, a return to activity, the window turns into a door.

Five of Swords

Bullying, stormy situations, hollow victory, one-upmanship.

Reversed: Negotiation, compromise, forgiveness, making amends.

Six of Swords

Transition, a guardian angel, rite of passage, moving away from troubled waters.

Reversed: Stuck, resistance to change, unfinished business, issues that need to be resolved before moving on.

Seven of Swords

Deception, dishonesty, underhandedness, someone or something negative that is living in our heads rent-free.

Reversed: Stealth, strategic approach, getting sound advice, resisting temptation.

Eight of Swords

Entrapment, self-affliction, victim mentality, feeling stuck even though we are free to walk away.

Reversed: Possibilities, liberation, moving forward, clearing obstacles.

Nine of Swords
Depression, anxiety, bad dreams, disturbance in our sleeping patterns.

Reversed: Recovery, the serenity prayer, restful sleep, coming out of a low point.

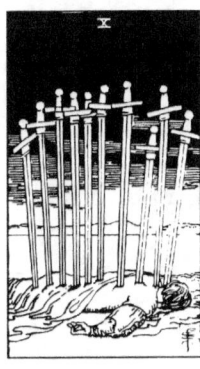

Ten of Swords
Breakdown, desolation, catastrophic thinking, being stabbed in the back.

Reversed: Recovery, regeneration, new horizons, the end of a cycle.

Page of Swords - Earth of Air
Investigation, being cautious, looking backward, thirst for knowledge.

Reversed: Spiteful, manipulative, defensive, all talk and no action.

Knight of Swords - Fire of Air

Swiftness, ambition, action-oriented, driven to succeed.

Reversed: Slowing down, thinking things through.
Adversely: Aggressive, fight or flight.

Queen of Swords - Water of Air

Thoughtful, intelligent, perceptive, in control of emotions.

Reversed: Bitchy, pessimist, cold-hearted, a powerful mind turned toward manipulation.

King of Swords - Air of Air

Analytical, decisive, confident, and mental clarity.

Reversed: Judgmental, arrogance, domineering, misuse of power.

Ace of Pentacles - Earth

Nature, abundance, wealth, material world.

Reversed: Financial blocks, poor investments, lost opportunity, lack of planning.

Two of Pentacles

Balance, multitasking, juggling responsibilities, adapting to circumstances.

Reversed: Imbalance, burdens, being overdrawn, unexpected obstacles.

Three of Pentacles

Teamwork, collaboration, skilled labor, master craftsman.

Reversed: Mediocrity, cutting corners, poor execution, unrewarding career.

Four of Pentacles

Greed, miserliness, hoarding, fear of risk.

Reversed: Spending, generosity, openness. Adversely: reckless spending.

Five of Pentacles

Hardship, material insecurity, feeling left out in the cold, the door may be open, but unwilling to go inside.

Reversed: Improving circumstances, relief from suffering, coming in from out of the cold, the window turns into a door.

Six of Pentacles

Giving, sharing, assistance, support.

Reversed: Receiving, self-care. Adversely: Power dynamics, strings attached.

Seven of Pentacles

Harvest, progress, perseverance, pause from work.

Reversed: Work resumed. Adversely: Impatience, procrastination, unfinished projects.

Eight of Pentacles

Apprenticeship, practice, dedication, slow but steady progress.

Reversed: Perfectionism, inadequate training, unrewarding work, dead-end job.

Nine of Pentacles

Abundance, luxury, self-sufficiency, financial independence.

Reversed: Superficiality, codependency, living beyond means, material instability.

Ten of Pentacles
Family, ancestors, inheritance, financial security.

Reversed: Materialism, hoarding wealth, family feuds, financial failure.

Page of Pentacles - Earth of Earth
Studious, dependable, hardworking, athletic prowess.

Reversed: Uncommitted, needed discipline, missed opportunities, moving from job to job.

Knight of Pentacles - Fire of Earth
Diligence, persistence, grounded, stick-to-itiveness.

Reversed: Obstacles, feeling stuck, burnout from work, risky investments.

Queen of Pentacles - Water of Earth

Nature, fertility, physical security, hearth and home.

Reversed: Materialistic, frivolous, possessive, keeping up appearances.

King of Pentacles - Air of Earth

Wealth, comfort, security, physical satisfaction.

Reversed: Materialism, irresponsibility, corruption, financially inept.

A Note on the Knights and Kings

Traditionally, Knights have been associated with the element of air, and Kings are associated with the element of fire. I've switched the two because it makes more sense astrologically. Also, I equate Knights as middle-aged, and Kings as older adults. As an older adult in my sixties, even though the fire is still there, I find myself being more cerebral. Because of this, I feel that Kings are a better match with the properties of air.

ABOUT THE AUTHOR

At the age of thirteen, Alan Dee Geddes discovered his first Tarot deck at a place called the Fun Shop, a magic and novelty store in Ogden, Utah. This began his fascination with cartomancy and the intuitive arts.

In 1996, he pursued Wicca as a spiritual path. One of its teachings is to acquire a Magickal tool. That was the inspiration he needed to continue his journey with Tarot, and has been reading cards professionally ever since.

A reading with Alan can incorporate angelic energies, cord cutting, chakra work, reiki, and a number of other modalities. He became a Reiki Master in 2018.

He keeps busy reading cards and teaching classes at several new age shops, markets, and conventions throughout Utah.

Alan can be reached at geddesmagic@gmail.com